# THE ART AND TECHNIQUE OF

# Decorating Eggs

### With thanks to Gabriella Szutor

FIRST PRIZE AT THE
SALON INTERNATIONAL DES OEUFS DECORES
1994 – COMPIEGNE

# SEARCH PRESS

# Contents

# Introduction

This book offers a wide range of techniques for decorating eggs. The different methods are explained clearly and simply, and each technique is illustrated with numerous photographs and line drawings to show the various stages involved. Each project is also accompanied by a life-size photograph showing variations on a particular theme. There is a large variety of projects to choose from. You can decorate your eggs using stencilling, collaging or scraperboard techniques; or you could be more adventurous and opt for sculpting or engraving.

The technical level required for each model varies, so it is best to begin with simple projects and to gradually proceed to more elaborate models. In this way, you will familiarise yourself with the various techniques involved in decorating eggs as you work. Remember that the success of your decorated eggs depends on the care and precision with which you work, so proceed with caution.

# General advice

## EQUIPMENT

This list includes all the equipment used in this book. You do not need all the items. Read through each project before you begin so that you know exactly what is required.

Pipette with a pump
1.5mm (¹/₁₆in) drill or round file
Saucepan
Sieve
Dye bath
Iron
Drafting pen
Propelling pencil
HB pencil
White crayon
Selection of paintbrushes
Toothbrush
Modelling stick

Craft knife
Razor blades
Small, sharp, pointed scissors
Needle
Beeswax
Candle
Tjanting
Soft eraser
Ultra-fine sandpaper
Old magazines
Decorative wrapping paper
Thin paper

Thin and thick card
Tracing paper
Paper towelling
Wallpaper paste
Air-drying clay
Indian ink
Acrylic or gouache paint
Cold-water batik dye
All-purpose glue
Spray varnish (matt)
Gloss varnish
Tape measure
Soft cloth
Piece of nylon stocking

Ribbon
String
Curtain rings
Acetate
Vinegar
Washing-up liquid
Cocktail stick
Polystyrene
Onion skins
Straw
Fine sand
Leaves or petals

1

## CHOOSING AN EGG

The essential factor to consider when choosing an egg, is the shell: it must be smooth and well-shaped. It is important to stress that only eggs from domestic fowl should be used. Many species of wild birds are now protected by law and their eggs should never be procured for the purposes of decoration.

## PREPARING AN EGG

All the projects in this book use 'blown' eggs – ones which have been emptied and cleaned. The blowing process, which uses a pipette and pump, avoids the risk of the contents rotting.

Place a soft cloth on your work surface to cushion the egg in case you drop it. Wipe over the shell with a mixture of washing-up liquid and water to remove all grease. Wipe very gently so as to avoid removing the natural enamel.

Carefully make a 1.5mm ($^1/_{16}$in) hole in the base of the egg using drill or a small, pointed round file (see photo 1).

Insert the tip of the pipette into the hole and then gently squeeze the pump (photo 2). Continue doing this until the egg is drained completely.

Use the pipette to carefully wash out the inside of the shell with a mixture of water and vinegar. Leave to dry.

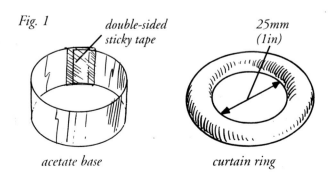

2

3

## SUPPORTING AN EGG

Support an egg between stages of decoration, on a cocktail stick stuck in a block of polystyrene (photo 3).

## DISPLAYING AN EGG

The best way to make an egg stand upright is to position it on a circular plastic, cardboard or wooden base. Curtain rings or little bases made from acetate or thin card are ideal for this purpose (fig 1).

*Fig. 1*    *double-sided sticky tape*    *25mm (1in)*

*acetate base*    *curtain ring*

# Dyeing with onions

## LEAF AND PETAL DESIGNS

In this project, leaves and petals are used to mask areas of the egg. The egg is then dyed and the colour of the shell is preserved underneath each leaf shape. This technique requires a large quantity of onion skins, so it is a good idea to save any that you use when cooking.

The colour of the dye depends on the number of onion skins used. The greater the quantity, the darker the dye will be. Many decorated eggs in this book are dyed using this method. If you use leaves or paper (see page 8) to mask the egg, the dye can be recycled.

1. Collect a number of small leaves and petals. Slightly dampen each leaf or petal, then apply them gently on to the surface of the egg.

2. Cover the entire egg with a piece of nylon stocking. Tighten the stocking by twisting the ends between thumb and forefinger. Tie with a piece of string (see above).

3. Fill a small saucepan with onion skins, cover with water and bring to the boil. Allow to simmer for about fifteen minutes.

4. Sieve the hot dye into a small container to remove the skins.

5. Check that the leaves are positioned correctly then totally immerse the egg in the dye solution (fig. 1). Leave for five to ten minutes, depending on the colour required: the longer you leave the egg in the dye for, the darker the colour will be. Turn the egg regularly. Allow to dry.

6. Apply a coat of varnish.

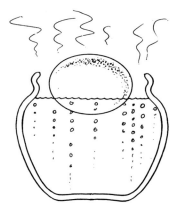

*Fig. 1*

## USING PAPER SHAPES

You can also mask the egg with a design cut from thin paper.

1. For a symmetrical design, fold the paper in four and cut the design with a pair of sharp, pointed scissors (see above).

2. Dampen the paper design, apply it to the egg and hold it in place with a piece of nylon stocking (see right).

8

# *Batik*

Batik is a magical technique that uses beeswax as a resist to the dye colour. Eggs decorated this way do not need to be varnished, as the beeswax itself leaves a sheen on the surface of the egg when it is wiped off.

In this project, a design is drawn lightly on to the egg and a wax line is then traced over it with a tjanting. The drawing must be very precise, so try a simple geometric design to begin with. Drawing on the curved surface of an egg is very different from drawing on flat paper, so practise first.

Use a pencil to outline the design on to the egg. If you prefer, you could use a pen, or a needle supported in a propelling pencil. The pencil lines can not be easily removed once the egg has been coloured. They should therefore be kept very light and only essential outlines and details should be sketched on.

1. Heat the tjanting over a candle flame and then scoop some beeswax into its reservoir (photo 1).

2. Melt the wax over the candle flame (photo 2). Block the spout with a piece of paper towelling.

3. Trace over the pencil lines on the egg with the spout of the tjanting. Try to get the lines of wax as even as possible (photo 3). Work slowly and carefully, as mistakes are very difficult to correct.

4. Make up a cold water batik dye following the manufacturer's instructions. Hot water will melt the wax and ruin the design. Immerse the wax-covered egg into a dye bath.

5. Check the development of the colour regularly and remove the egg from the dye bath when the desired colour is obtained. If you want several shades of colour, work from the lightest to the darkest. Preserve the lighter shades with a covering of wax and then repeat the process. Allow the egg to dry thoroughly between each dyeing. Continue until the design is complete.

6. Hold the egg near a candle flame until the wax starts to melt. Carefully wipe it off using a soft cloth. Continue until all the wax is removed (photo 4).

1

2

3

4

1    2    3    4

# *Scraperboard technique*

The designs engraved on the group of eggs opposite are created by scraping away layers of applied colour with the point of a craft knife or a sharp needle tool.

1. First, colour the whole of the egg shell using onion dye (see pages 6–8). Leave the eggs in the dye bath until a medium brown shade is obtained (photo 1). Allow to dry.

2. Paint in part of the shell with an even layer of Indian ink. Choose a simple shape such as a diamond, oval, circle or stripe (photo 2). Leave to dry.

3. Sketch a design over the inked shape using a sharp white crayon. Do not press too hard.

4. Use your craft knife or needle tool to scrape along the white outlines (see below). This will remove the ink and reveal the background colour.

5. Scratch the main outline of the design first (photo 3) and then work in the detail (photo 4). If you scrape the Indian ink away gently, you will reveal the background colour. If you scratch harder, you will reveal the natural colour of the shell. Use both methods to create different shades and effects. If you make a mistake, correct it using more Indian ink. Leave to dry before you attempt to scratch into it again.

As a variation on this project, you could colour the background using a solution of Indian ink and water-based paint rather than the dye bath to create a delicate random pattern (see page 32). Let your imagination go and scrape a design directly on to the background colour without sketching it in first. The eggs on page 14 have all been decorated using this technique.

# Collage

## PATCHWORK DESIGNS

You may think that it is impossible to cover the curved surface of an egg with flat pieces of paper, but by using small, carefully cut out shapes, an entire egg can be completely and flawlessly covered.

1. Collect decorative wrapping paper and pictures from magazines.

2. Cut out shapes and brush the back of each piece with wallpaper paste (see right).

3. Assemble the pieces of paper so that they do not overlap. The wallpaper paste allows the paper to stretch, making it easier to position each piece on a curved surface. Continue building up a collage until the entire egg is covered. Leave to dry.

4. Use a drafting pen to draw on fine lines to suggest seams and the effect of patchwork.

*BELOW: Use thick card to construct an attractive gift box and then decorate it to complement your egg. The box will protect the egg and make it easier to transport. Secure the egg on a circular base (see page 5).*

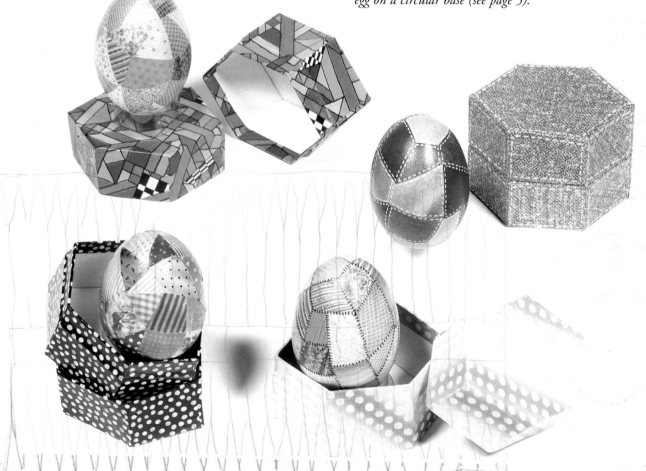

## SEGMENTED COLLAGE

The success of this technique depends upon accurate cutting out. It is also important to position the collage carefully on the egg. It is virtually impossible to avoid the occasional overlap, so use thin paper so that the surface does not get ridges in it. If you select a glossy paper for this project, your model should not need varnishing.

1. Measure the egg you intend to decorate using a tape measure. The measurements you need are the curve of the height (A) and the circumference at the widest part of the egg (B) (see fig. 1).

2. Draw a rectangle based on these measurements on tracing paper. Place the rectangle over your picture and move it into position. Try to get unimportant elements of design, such as sky or foliage for example, at the very top or bottom of the grid, as these sections may later be overlapped or cut into. Position important details, such as faces for example, as near as possible to the central band.

3. Cut out the rectangle from the picture. Draw a grid, similar to fig. 2 on to the back of the picture, making each segment approximately 5mm (¹/₄in).

4. Cut each segment to a tapered point (photo 1). Cut out groups of three segments, leaving them attached to the central band.

5. Brush the back of each group with wallpaper paste. Position them in turn on to the egg (photo 2). Continue adding three-segment groups until the entire egg is covered. Leave to dry. Paper contracts as it dries, so any small wrinkles should disappear.

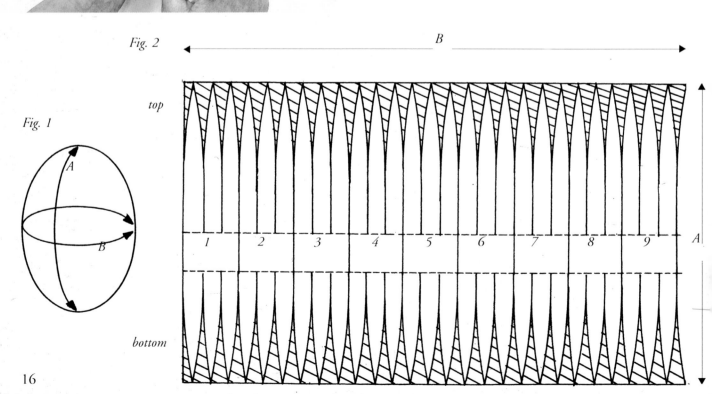

*Fig. 2*

B

*top*

*Fig. 1*

A

1 2 3 4 5 6 7 8 9

A

*bottom*

# Drawing in pencil

This technique is suitable for a wide range of designs. You could choose to create stylized figures (see page 20), or you may opt for a more abstract design (see opposite). The shell must be immaculate if you are going to draw directly in pencil on to it, so try to choose smooth eggs, such as hen or duck eggs. If you use a goose egg, rub it gently with ultra-fine sandpaper before you start as the shell can often be slightly rough.

1. Sketch the outline of your design on to the egg using an HB pencil. Remember to sharpen your pencil regularly, so that the point is always sharp. Gently hold the egg in a cloth and try not to touch or rub sections already drawn. Remove any mistakes by gently scraping with a craft knife, rather than using an eraser.

2. Gradually add the details. Work in the shadows, and leave the egg shell bare for the highlights. You can enhance the natural tone of the egg by adding colour washes in the same range, such as light beige, ivory or pale pink (see page 21).

3. Fix the drawing by spraying with matt varnish.

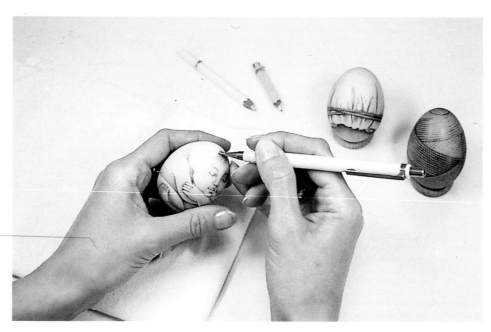

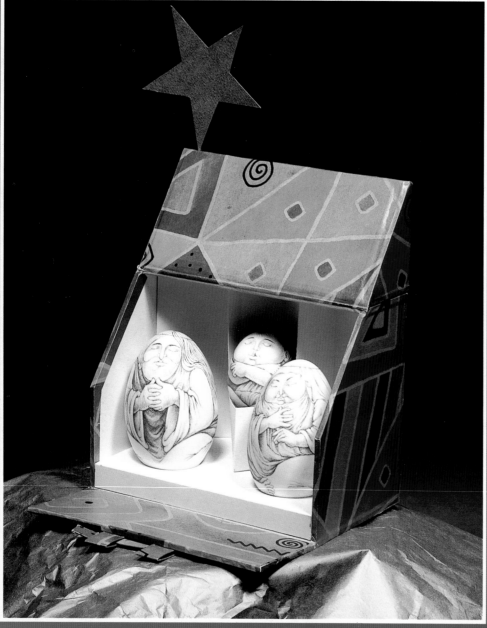

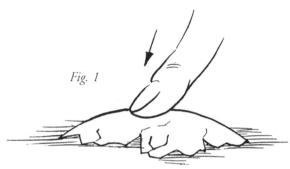

*Fig. 1*

# *Mosaics*

Shells are broken into tiny pieces for this project and these are then applied as a mosaic on to another egg. You can use natural or coloured pieces, and you can work on a natural or coloured background shell. As a general rule, best results are obtained by using light or medium coloured pieces on a dark background or vice-versa.

1. Colour the outside of large pieces of egg shell using either paint, Indian ink or dye, or leave the shell uncoloured if you prefer.

2. Break the bits of shell into small pieces by pressing on the top of the curve with your finger (fig 1).

3. Use a crayon to lightly mark a design on to the egg you want to decorate.

4. Carefully cover both sides of a piece of shell with varnish then use a needle fitted into a propelling pencil to pick the piece up.

5. Place the piece on the surface of the egg and gently slide it into position (see above). Continue to stick on pieces until the surface of the egg is covered. There is no need to varnish the finished egg, as all the individual pieces of shell will be shiny as they have already been coated (see left).

# Applying straw

This is one of the simplest techniques, and is suitable for beginners. You do not need to be good at drawing to decorate eggs with straw, you just need to be able to arrange the pieces of straw into an attractive pattern.

For this project, varnish is used as glue to attach the straw to the egg shell.

1. Cut the stalks of straw into 100mm (4in) lengths. Soak them in water for forty-eight hours.

2. Open each length of straw along its length using a craft knife (fig 1).

3. Remove the pith from the inside of the stalk with a razor blade (fig 2).

4. Iron the stalks flat using a warm iron.

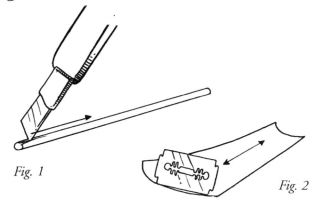

*Fig. 1*

*Fig. 2*

*Fig. 3*

5. Colour the surface of the egg using paint, ink or dye. The shade should be quite dark so that it will contrast with the colour of the straw.

6. Use a pencil to divide the egg up into segments relating to your design (see fig. 4).

7. Use a small pair of scissors to cut the straw into shapes to fit into your segments (fig. 3 and photo left).

8. Varnish the pith side of the straw pieces and place them on the design using a needle fixed in a propelling pencil. Apply the straw to the egg following the outline of the design (see below). Continue, until the egg is decorated all over.

9. Apply a coat of varnish. Leave to dry.

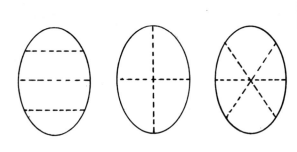

*Fig. 4*

# Modelling with air-drying clay

The two essential stages involved in working with air-drying clay are the modelling of the clay shapes and the positioning of each piece on the egg. Air-drying clay is available in several colours, which means that you can build up multi-coloured designs. You should treat your finished egg with extra care as the raised design is quite fragile.

1. Sketch out your design ideas on a piece of paper. Mark the essential points of your design on to the egg so that you can gauge the size and number of pieces to be modelled. If you have designed a frieze to go all around the egg, measure the circumference of the egg and then divide it by the number of elements in your frieze so that the design is regular and you can join the two ends of the frieze accurately.

2. Use acrylic paint to colour the background of your egg. If you use a pale colour, the outline of your design should still show through. Allow to dry.

3. Make the little shapes for your design in air-drying clay by modelling them with a craft knife, a modelling stick or just with your fingers (see left). Do not make bulky pieces as they will stick out on the finished egg and are therefore liable to break off easily.

4. Check that all the pieces are exactly the right size before leaving them in the air to harden (check the manufacturer's instructions for drying times). When hardened, the pieces are fragile and cannot be remodelled.

5. Stick all the clay decorations on to the egg using all-purpose craft glue (see below).

6. Apply a coat of varnish.

# Indian ink designs

There are lots of possibilities for designs using Indian ink, but most fall into one of two categories: imaginative irregular designs or geometric patterns. You should initially select a design that is fairly simple to achieve and progress to models of increasing difficulty.

Delicate symmetrical designs such as the dragonfly on page 1, require a high standard of drawing and they must be carefully planned. Imaginative, freer designs featuring flowers, leaves, waves and mosaic patterns for example, can be drawn freehand directly on to the egg after the background colour has been applied. Use a drafting pen or a fine paintbrush to do this. Geometric patterns require careful planning. This project uses a simple criss-cross pattern and requires a very smooth shell to work on (see page 18), so choose your egg carefully.

1. Transfer the grid for the pattern on to the egg using a sharp lead pencil. Do not press too hard (photo 1). Ensure that the grid on the egg is as accurate as possible, as it is difficult to make corrections once the Indian ink has been applied.

2. Fill in the design using Indian ink (photo 2).

3. Carefully rub out the pencil grid lines using a soft eraser.

4. Apply a coat of varnish.

1

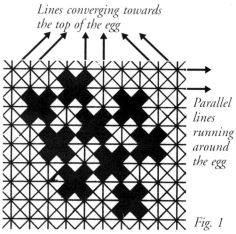

*Lines converging towards the top of the egg*

*Parallel lines running around the egg*

Fig. 1

2

# Painted effects

Use acrylic or gouache paints to colour your eggs. Experiment first, to ensure that the paint you have chosen will provide an even covering of colour. Acrylic paint is particularly good if you want to apply one colour on top of another. The technique of decorating eggs using paint is one of the most accessible for beginners, and it can be adapted to suit all artistic tastes. The examples below show patterns that you could use or adapt.

1. Support the egg on a cocktail stick (see page 5). Paint in a background colour. Leave to dry.

2. Use a pencil to lightly sketch in the outline of your design.

3. Paint in your design carefully. Leave to dry.

4. Acrylic and gouache paints dry with a matt finish, so apply a coat of varnish to the decorated egg.

# Mixing ink and paint

Indian ink and water-based paint are here used together in a technique that exploits the fact that these two mediums do not mix. This is an exciting technique as the results are often unpredictable and always unique. The mixture of ink and paint will colour the surface irregularly to produce effects that range from mottled and marbled to dribbled and textured. This is a simple technique as it does not involve any drawing or planning. However, it is still worth practising, so you become familiar with the effects that are possible.

1. Support the egg on a cocktail stick (see page 5).

2. Mix up your paint with a little water. Use a paintbrush to dab the top of the egg with paint. Allow the paint to run down to the bottom of the egg.

3. Continue, building up other colours. Turn the egg from time to time to change the direction of flow of the paint, or use a paintbrush to merge the colours.

4. Apply Indian ink on top of the paint while it is still wet. Use the same technique as above to build up colours. Leave to dry.

5. Apply a coat of varnish to brighten up your colours.

# *Using vinegar*

## SURFACE ENGRAVING

This technique uses no dye or paint. The different colours are achieved by the bleaching and corrosive action of vinegar. The monochrome effect is very delicate. The darkest tone is the shell, and all the other tones are achieved by immersing the egg in vinegar for different lengths of time. The lightest areas are those which have been immersed for longest.

1. Use a pencil to mark the first elements of your design on to the surface of the egg.

2. Apply resist lines of beeswax very carefully (see above and page 10). Remember that the original colour of the shell will be preserved where you put the wax. Do not worry about covering up the sketch lines as they will disappear during the bleaching process.

3. Block the hole where you emptied the egg with a small amount of wax. Totally immerse the egg into a jar of vinegar (see left). Leave for ten minutes to two hours, depending on how light a shade you want to obtain, and how deep the engraving. Turn the egg regularly.

4. Rinse the egg in water and allow to dry. Do not remove the wax lines.

5. Sketch on more elements of your design and add more resist lines of wax. As before, you should put the wax over the areas where you want the colour to be retained. Continue building up layers of wax and immersing in vinegar until you are happy with your design.

6. Remove the wax as shown on page 10 (see also right).

## CREATING HOLES

This method utilizes the corrosive action of vinegar to create holes in the shell. The vinegar is left on for much longer than in the surface engraving technique, so that it totally rather than partially corrodes the shell. Beeswax is used as a resist to protect areas of the shell and so form the design. You should think carefully about your design before you start, as the wax cannot be removed once it has been applied.

1. Draw on the outlines of the design using a pencil (photo 1).

2. Apply the beeswax as shown on page 34 (photo 2).

3. Place your egg in a jar of vinegar. Leave for two to ten hours, depending on the thickness of the shell (photo 3).

4. Although the shell will disintegrate, the internal membrane is resistant to the effect of vinegar and will therefore remain intact. Remove this membrane with a craft knife as shown left (see photo also 4).

5. Decorate the egg by painting areas in a solid colour, and then flicking with paint in a contrasting colour (photo 5). To do this, use an old toothbrush, as shown below. Flick the bristles away from you using a flat, rigid object such as a set square.

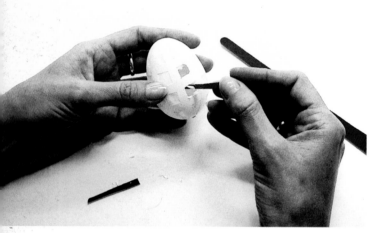

1

2

3

4

5

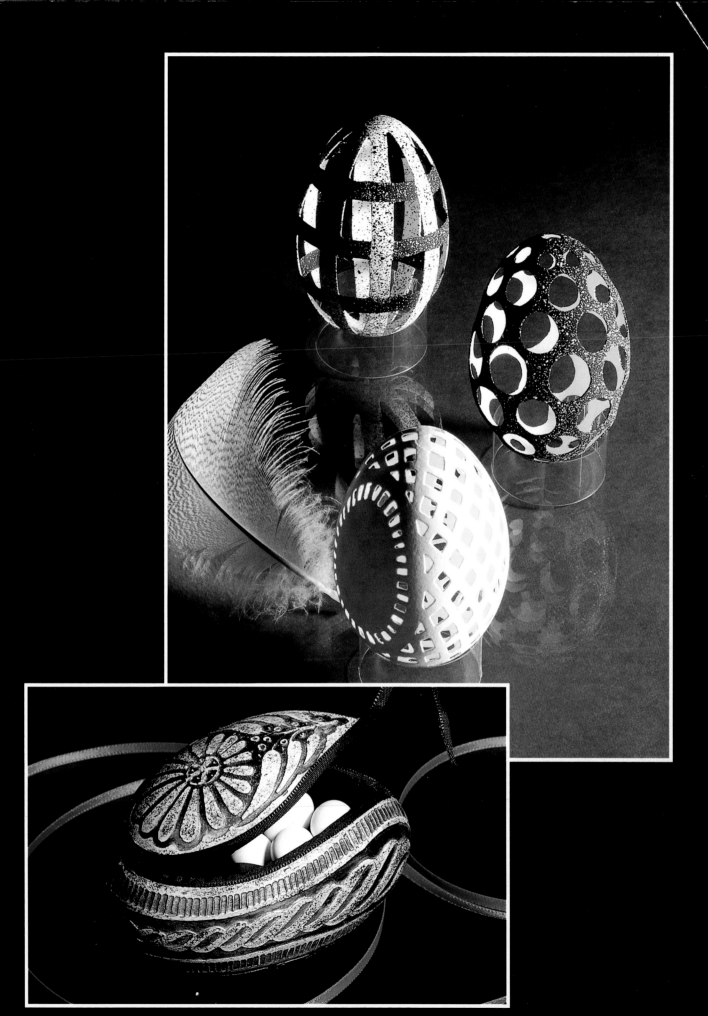

## SWIRLING CAVITIES

These stunning holes are achieved by
corroding large areas of the shell with
vinegar. Beeswax acts as a resist to protect
the main part of the shell. This technique
requires patience, but the results are worth
it. The finished eggs are extremely fragile,
so handle them very carefully. This project
uses the natural colour of the egg as the
background, but you could choose to
colour it before you begin.

1

2

1. Sketch swirling holes on to the shell and then use
the technique shown on page 36 to corrode areas
away.

2. Wrap extra-fine sandpaper around a pencil or
crayon and, working very gently, sand the edges of the
swirling cavities until they are smooth (photo 1).

3. Use a pencil to sketch a series of swirling lines on to
the shell. Work with the contours of the egg and the
shape of the holes (photo 2).

4. Use black Indian ink to fill in the pencil lines to
produce striking stripes.

5. Apply a coat of varnish. This will strengthen the
shell and will enrich the painted areas.

## MAKING LIDS

You can also use the vinegar technique to separate part
of the shell for use as a lid (see the model at the
bottom of page 37).

1. Draw an unbroken line around the area of the shell
that you want to remove.

2. Cover the egg with wax, being careful not to paint
over the pencil line.

3. Immerse the egg in vinegar until the line has cor-
roded. Cut through the membrane with a craft knife.
The egg will then divide into two parts.

4. Glue ribbon around the edges of the shell and lid to
make an attractive join. Leave a length of ribbon on
the lid to act as a handle.

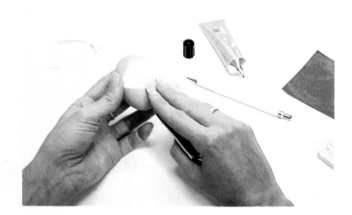

# Sculpting

This technique again uses wax resist and vinegar to make holes in the shell. These holes are then filled in using thin card to create the illusion that the eggs have been sculpted. For more elaborate models, you can divide the shell up completely (see page 38), and then reconstruct the egg using card. This technique is used for the model at the top of the opposite page. The pieces of shell have been filled with circles of card and then the layers supported in the middle by cylinders of card. The model on the middle right of the photograph uses circles of shell joined back together by small dots of glue.

1. Sketch the shape you want to cut out (photo 1).

2. Use wax resist and vinegar to corrode away the hole as shown on page 36 (see also photo 2). Lightly sand the edges of the shell (see page 38).

3. Fold a piece of card in half, then place it into the hole. Use a sharp pencil to mark the shape of the hole on to the card, as shown top left.

4. Cut the card along the pencil line as shown middle left.

5. Fit the cut-out shape over the opening in the egg and then stick it in place using multi-purpose glue (photo 3). Leave the glue to dry.

6. Gently sand the join using ultra-fine sandpaper, as shown left.

7. Use the technique shown on page 36 to create the impression of stone. Flick white paint over black and vice versa (photo 4).

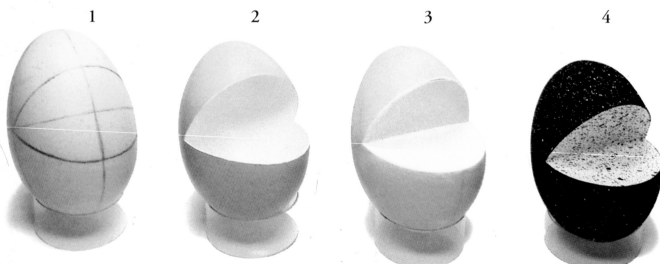

1         2         3         4

# *Texturing with sand*

This simple technique involves covering all or part of the surface of the egg with fine sand to create a textured appearance. It can be combined with other methods of decoration, such as engraving. The engraving should be done before the sand is applied. If you wish to emphasise the texture of the sand, use a single colour on the egg, preferably a dark one. The four eggs opposite show the effectiveness of this approach.

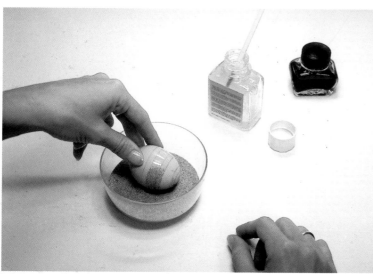

1. Decide which areas you want to cover with sand and then pencil an outline of your design on to the egg.

2. Brush varnish or glue on to the areas that you want to cover with sand (see above).

3. Roll the egg in a small bowl of sand. The sand will stick to the varnished areas (see left). Leave to dry.

4. Brush off any excess sand using a paint-brush.

5. Paint the entire surface of the egg, including the areas covered with sand, using Indian ink or paint (see below left). Allow to dry.

6. Apply a coat of varnish to the bare shell. This will emphasise the difference in texture between the shell and the areas covered in sand.

# Creative ideas

This chapter contains fun and imaginative suggestions for decorating eggs, using a mixture of the techniques shown so far. You can combine simple techniques to create stunning and original designs such as rugby balls, suitcases or jigsaw puzzles.

Use these and other decorated eggs featured in the book to inspire you to create your own work. You can adapt any of the models or techniques shown to make exceptional and unique gifts for friends and family.

## RUGBY BALLS

For this project, painting and wax techniques are combined to create an authentic-looking rugby ball. It is important that the outline is accurate or the effect will not be as convincing.

1. Measure the egg then divide it up into the various parts that make up a rugby ball. Mark on the outline with a pencil.

2. Fill each area evenly with small dots of beeswax to create the texture of the ball (photo 1). Do not go over the pencil lines with the dots. Leave to dry.

3. Paint over the surface of the egg using acrylic or gouache paint (photo 2). Leave to dry.

4. Add the details using white paint or black Indian ink. Paint the seams in the lines left between the dots of wax.

The soccer balls shown on the opposite page use a complex octagonal grid. They have been shaded with pencil directly on the shell and the seams are added afterwards in black Indian ink.

1

2

## BRICKS

These eggs use the technique of surface engraving shown on page 34 to create the mortar. The bricks themselves are the colour of the natural shell, but you could use gouache or acrylic paint to colour them. This project shows how effective it can be to adapt a technique to suit a particular theme.

## JIGSAW PUZZLES

The technique used here is the paint and ink method shown on page 32. Once the background is coloured, you can draw in the outline of the puzzle pieces using black Indian ink. Highlight the edges of the pieces using white paint.

## SUITCASES

These eggs are painted all over with black Indian ink. Beeswax is then used to make the straps and handles. The wax can either be left its natural colour or it can be painted when dry. Add the labels using the collage technique shown on page 15. The little trunk also pictured is constructed out of card.

# Index

First published in Great Britain 1998 by
Search Press Limited
Wellwood, North Farm Road, Tunbridge Wells, Kent TN2 3DR

Originally published in France 1996 by
Éditions Didier CARPENTIER
Original title: *Arts et Techniques des Oeufs Décorés*
Copyright © Éditions Didier CARPENTIER 1997

English translation by Judith Aymé
English translation © Search Press Limited 1998

ISBN 0 85532 865 7

Printed in Spain by Elkar S. Coop. Bilbao 48012